My New Home
After Iran

CRABTREE
PUBLISHING COMPANY
WWW.CRABTREEBOOKS.COM

Heather C. Hudak

CRABTREE
PUBLISHING COMPANY
WWW.CRABTREEBOOKS.COM

Author: Heather C. Hudak

Editors: Sarah Eason, Harriet McGregor, and Janine Deschenes

Proofreader and indexer: Wendy Scavuzzo

Editorial director: Kathy Middleton

Design: Paul Myerscough and Jessica Moon

Photo research: Rachel Blount

Production coordinator and Prepress technician: Ken Wright

Print coordinator: Katherine Berti

Consultant: Hawa Sabriye

Written, developed, and produced by Calcium

Publisher's Note: The story presented in this book is a fictional account based on extensive research of real-life accounts by refugees, with the aim of reflecting the true experience of refugee children and their families.

Photo Credits:
t=Top, c=Center, b=Bottom, l= Left, r=Right

Cover: Shutterstock

Inside: Jessica Moon: p. 29b; Shutterstock: Leonid Andronov: p. 6-7c; Koldunova Anna: p. 1l; Artskvortsova: p. 8bl; Astudio: p. 16t; J Bar: p. 22b; Bistraffic: p. 16bl; ChameleonsEye: pp. 15l, 16c, 24; Curioso: p. 7t; Gabdrakipova Dilyara: p. 18c; Elenabsl: pp. 18bl, 23tr, 26bl; EQRoy: p. 25; Anna Frajtova: p. 24t; Hennadii H: p. 5br; Dave Hewison Photography: p. 29cl; IsoVector: p. 19r; Pojana Jermsawat: p. 21; Julinzy: p. 4tr; Jane Kelly: p. 8l; Helga Khorimarko: p. 21l; Lawkeeper: p. 15t; Loveshop: p. 5cl; Nicola Messana Photos: p. 20; Mspoint: p. 28t; Elena Odareeva: p. 5cr, 28b; Olyvia: p. 18t; Paintings: pp. 9t, 12-13c, 14b; Rawpixel.com: pp. 26-27; Saeediex: p. 6b; Sera57: p. 1bg; Sirtravelalot: p. 19t; Sudowoodo: pp. 3, 5tr, 29t; Darren Tierney: p. 13b; Grant Tiffen: p. 17b; What's My Name: p. 14t; Victor Wong: p. 22t; Yutthana-landscape: p. 10b; Zstock: p. 27t; Zurijeta: p. 23l; Wikimedia Commons: J Bar: p. 22b; DIAC images: p. 10t.

Library and Archives Canada Cataloguing in Publication

Title: My new home after Iran / Heather C. Hudak.
Names: Hudak, Heather C., 1975- author.
Series: Leaving my homeland: after the journey.
Description: Series statement: Leaving my homeland: after the journey | Includes index.
Identifiers: Canadiana (print) 20190114878 | Canadiana (ebook) 20190114894 | ISBN 9780778765011 (softcover) | ISBN 9780778764953 (hardcover) | ISBN 9781427123756 (HTML)
Subjects: LCSH: Refugees—Iran—Juvenile literature. | LCSH: Refugees—Australia—Juvenile literature. | LCSH: Refugee children—Iran—Juvenile literature. | LCSH: Refugee children—Australia—Juvenile literature. | LCSH: Refugees—Social conditions—Juvenile literature. | LCSH: Iran—History—1997—Juvenile literature. | LCSH: Iran—Social conditions—Juvenile literature.
Classification: LCC HV640.5.I73 H83 2019 | DDC j305.23086/9140955—dc23

Library of Congress Cataloging-in-Publication Data

Names: Hudak, Heather C., 1975- author.
Title: My new home after Iran / Heather C. Hudak.
Description: New York : Crabtree Publishing Company, [2019] | Series: Leaving my homeland: after the journey | Includes index.
Identifiers: LCCN 2019023038 (print) | LCCN 2019023039 (ebook) | ISBN 9780778764953 (hardcover) | ISBN 9780778765011 (paperback) | ISBN 9781427123756 (ebook)
Subjects: LCSH: Refugees--Iran--Juvenile literature. | Refugees--Australia--Juvenile literature. | Refugee children--Iran--Juvenile literature. | Refugee children--Australia--Juvenile literature.
Classification: LCC HV640.5.I73 H829 2019 (print) | LCC HV640.5.I73 (ebook) | DDC 362.7/79140899155094--dc23
LC record available at https://lccn.loc.gov/2019023038
LC ebook record available at https://lccn.loc.gov/2019023039

Crabtree Publishing Company
www.crabtreebooks.com   1-800-387-7650

Printed in the U.S.A./082019/CG20190712

Published in Canada
Crabtree Publishing
616 Welland Ave.
St. Catharines, Ontario
L2M 5V6

Published in the United States
Crabtree Publishing
PMB 59051
350 Fifth Avenue, 59th Floor
New York, New York 10118

Published in the United Kingdom
Crabtree Publishing
Maritime House
Basin Road North, Hove
BN41 1WR

Published in Australia
Crabtree Publishing
Unit 3 – 5 Currumbin Court
Capalaba
QLD 4157

What Is in This Book?

Zahra's Story: My New Home in Australia

Hi! My name is Zahra. I live in Brisbane, Australia. I have lived here 10 years. I even started classes at the University of Brisbane this year! I want to work in the government one day so I can help influence **immigration policies**. I like my life in Australia. But life has not been easy. I was a **refugee** from Iran.

My family and I fled Iran because we were afraid for our safety. In Iran, the government wants to control the actions of its people. Women must dress a certain way in public. Many TV shows and movies are banned. People cannot even dance. When people speak against the government, they can be arrested or killed.

Australia's flag

Turkey

Caspian Sea

Tehran

Syria

Afghanistan

Iraq

Iran

Jordan

Tehran is the capital of Iran. It is located in the northern part of the country.

Pakistan

India

Saudi Arabia

Persian Gulf

Gulf of Oman

UN Rights of the Child

A child's family has the responsibility to help make sure the child's **rights** are protected, and to help them learn to use their rights. While you read through this book, think about these rights.

Iran's flag

Like women, girls in Iran must dress in a certain way and wear headscarves when in public.

*We had to leave because my brother, Ahmad, spoke against the government on a **blog**. Some of his friends were arrested for doing the same. My parents warned him to stop. But then, he spoke with a reporter about his views. My parents feared for his life. We left before the newspaper story came out. We had no choice. I was just nine years old at the time. It was a dangerous journey to Australia. After a year in a **detention center**, we were **resettled** in Brisbane. I like my life here, but I still miss my friends and family back home every day.*

My Homeland, Iran

Most people in Iran practice the religion Islam. Religion is an important part of daily life, and Muslims pray several times each day. Since 1979, Iran has been ruled by religious leaders. They are very strict. They limit the rights and freedoms of people living in Iran.

People are not free to practice any religion. They cannot share their views on the government. They cannot gather in protest. Reporters and bloggers are often jailed. Many websites, such as Facebook and YouTube, have been blocked to keep people from connecting with the outside world. Musicians have even been arrested during concerts. Women and people with disabilities are treated poorly. The **LGBTQ** community is also treated badly. The lifestyle of LGBTQ people does not fit with the government's strict religious beliefs. LGBTQ people are often arrested. Trials are not fair, and people receive harsh punishments. Some are killed.

Over the past 200 years, Tehran has grown into a major city with a population of about 8.7 million.

The president of Iran, Hassan Rouhani, has promised to make changes that would improve people's lives. But little has changed under his leadership.

The Imamzadeh Saleh mosque is found in Tajrish Square in Tehran.

Iran has large amounts of valuable oil and gas. But the United States, United Kingdom, and other countries limit **trade** with Iran. These countries believe Iran's government supports **terrorism** in parts of the world.

Terrorism is a threat to Iran, too. Most attacks are due to differences in religious beliefs. The government is mainly Shia Muslim. Sunni Muslims are often treated poorly. The Islamic State in Iraq and Syria (ISIS) is a Sunni terrorist group. It believes the Shia should not be in power. ISIS has carried out attacks in Iran to try to gain power.

Story in Numbers

In Iran, about

35 percent

of the people are Persian. The name comes from the original name of Iran: Persia. Nearly 16 percent of the people are Azerbaijani. Kurds make up about 13 percent of the Iranian population. These are the three largest **ethnic groups** in Iran.

Zahra's Story: Leaving My Homeland

We left home so quickly that it felt like a whirlwind. I remember the panic I felt like it was yesterday. In days, my parents sold everything we had. We needed the money to get out of Iran quickly. We got on the first flight we could take to Jakarta in Indonesia.

When we arrived in Jakarta, a man took us to a house. Three weeks later, we were driven for hours to reach a beach. There, we paid the **smuggler** for his help, and for fake passports. Then we got into a boat with a lot of other people.

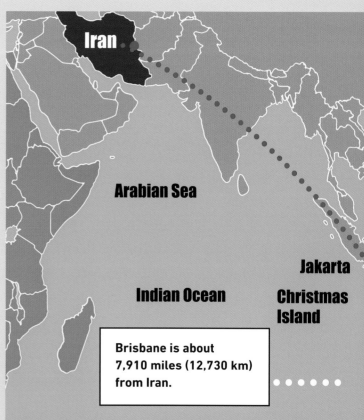

Iran

Arabian Sea

Jakarta

Indian Ocean

Christmas Island

Brisbane is about 7,910 miles (12,730 km) from Iran.

Story in Numbers

Australia resettles
more than

6,000

refugees each year.

These people are protesting against sending refugees to detention centers like the one on Manus Island. They argue that refugees should not be placed in detention centers, as though they are criminals.

Manus
Island

Indonesia

Australia

Brisbane

The boat journey was very difficult, and we were all really scared. We knew that we were in terrible danger. We were lucky to make it to shore on Christmas Island. But when we got there, we were told that we could not stay. We were then put on a plane to Manus Island in Papua New Guinea.

On Manus Island, we were sent to a detention center. It was like a prison. We lived in a huge room with many other people. There were no windows. When it was time to eat, we had to wait in line outside for hours. I hated Manus and could not wait to leave. After 12 long months, we found out Australia would take us in. My mother cried with joy. I could not wait to get there.

A New Life

Some refugees first come as visitors to Australia. After they arrive, they apply for **refugee status**. They wait in Australia to find out if they will be accepted. If they are accepted, they are helped by the Humanitarian Settlement Program (HSP). They are helped by **caseworkers** and provided with such things as basic supplies, English classes, and health care services.

But many other refugees arrive without the proper paperwork. They usually need to leave their country fast because of danger. However, Australia does not want to settle people who arrive illegally. The country wants to put off illegal refugees from making the boat journey to Australia. So, illegal refugees are sent to detention centers. The centers are on nearby islands in the South Pacific. Thousands of refugees live in the small centers.

As many as 30 people lived in each of the tents at the Manus Island detention center. They slept in bunk beds, and hung sheets between them for privacy.

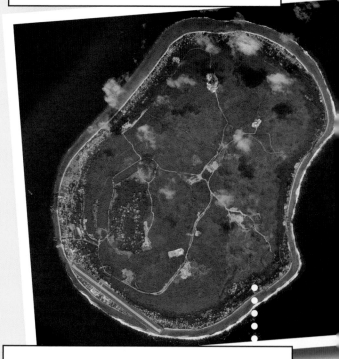

The island country of Nauru is just 3.5 miles (5.6 km) wide. The tiny island is poorly equipped to cope with the approximately 1,000 refugees who live in centers there.

Refugees are kept in the detention centers while they wait to find out if they will receive refugee status and be sent to a **host country** to live. They do not know how long this will take.

The detention center on Manus Island was officially closed in October 2017 because it was found to be unsafe. Some of the refugees were sent to newer centers in Papua New Guinea. But there are still hundreds of refugees on the island. They have few basic services and nowhere else to go. Human rights organizations have said that the people there live under cruel conditions. Many of them have harmed themselves or even tried to kill themselves. Their futures are uncertain.

Story in Numbers

When Manus Island closed,

606

refugees were stranded. Of them,

440

were granted refugee status by Australia. But Australia will not allow anyone to enter who arrives by boat. More than half of the remaining detainees were not given refugee status. About 50 others refused to process their applications as a way of protesting against being detained there.

Zahra's Story: Arriving in Brisbane

I feel so grateful that my family spent only one year in the detention center. I have heard about refugees who are in centers for years. Some children have lived their whole lives in them. They do not know what it is like to run and play in a park or go to a real school.

We were very lucky to be sent to live in Brisbane. It is in the state of Queensland. There were a lot of opportunities for us to build a happy life. But we missed Iran. For the first year, my mother cried in the night because she felt so badly for the family and friends we had left behind.

Since the 1980s, Australians have celebrated Refugee Week and World Refugee Day on June 20.

UN Rights of the Child

You have the right to special protection and help if you are a refugee.

Dear Yasmin,
I wish you could see Australia! When we arrived, our caseworker was so kind. She came to Australia as a refugee from Iran when she was a child. She had worked with a lot of families from Iran. We met some of them. It was nice to meet people who spoke our language. But it was still hard to adapt to our new life. Now, Brisbane feels like home. I would love to show it to you someday! Zahra

My father blamed my brother for the move. They argued a lot when they first arrived. My sister, Anahita, was angry, too. She had just started high school when we left Iran. She was making new friends and enjoyed her classes. She did not want to start over in a new school.

We were all jumpy for a long time after we settled into our new home. We were really scared that the government of Iran may have tracked us down. Every time we heard a knock on the door, we thought they had sent someone to take my brother away. We know now we are safe, and that would never happen to us.

Story Bridge was built in the 1930s. It is one of the best-known sites in Brisbane.

13

A New Home

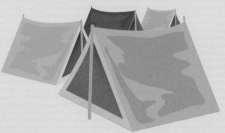

Many refugees flee their **homeland** with nothing. They often take long and dangerous journeys to escape. They may then live in detention centers. Offshore Australian detention centers are often compared to prisons. They do not have proper schools, and houses are in poor shape. The centers are dirty and diseases are common. Refugees are often attacked by locals if they leave the centers to get food or seek medical services. Many locals do not want the refugees on their island because they see them as a drain on their services.

Refugees that arrive by boat are not resettled in Australia. They are forced to stay in offshore centers, return to their homeland, or wait to see if another country will accept them. They cannot get jobs or build a safe, new life. Their only hope of a better future is to be sent to live in another part of the world.

Many refugees in detention centers face mental health problems. They feel hopeless for their future. Often, they do not get the help they need to cope.

UN Rights of the Child

You have the right to practice your own **culture**, language, and religion—or any you choose.

In larger Australian cities, such as Brisbane, there may be other refugee families who understand the experience of being a refugee.

Even for refugees who are resettled in Australia, it can be hard to start a new life. Most have no friends or family to help them. In larger cities, there may be other refugee families who understand the experience of being a refugee. In smaller cities and towns, there may not be any other refugee families or people who share their culture.

The government of Australia tries to settle refugees in communities in which they will have the best chance of being successful. The government looks for places with a lot of job opportunities. It also considers if there are other people who have the same culture or beliefs.

Zahra's Story: My New Home

I remember when we first got to Brisbane. We had nothing of our own. The government gave us a **crisis payment**. We used the money to buy clothes, furniture, food, and other things. After that, we got monthly payments to help us live until my parents could get jobs of their own. It was not much, but we got by.

I remember thinking how different Brisbane was from Tehran. There are people here from all backgrounds. I was surprised to learn that in some parts of Brisbane, nearly half of the people were born overseas. Everyone is free to practice their beliefs. The people here are friendly and easygoing.

In Iran, people often buy their food fresh each day from small stores like this one, or from the market. In Brisbane, they mainly shop in grocery stores.

Some Muslim women dress differently from Australian locals. They cover more of their body.

Story in Numbers

The people of Queensland come from more than

220

countries. They speak more than 180 languages and practice more than 110 religions.

16

I dress differently from the girls here. I cover my head with a **hijab** and I always wear long sleeves and pants. In Iran, it was not thought to be proper to show much skin. I still feel more comfortable this way. In Brisbane, women often wear shorts and tank tops. It is sunny and warm year round. At first, some of the kids at school teased me about the way I dressed. Then my teacher asked me to talk about my culture in class one day. After that, the other children wanted to know more about Iran and my culture.

The food in Australia is very different, too. We ate a lot of rice and flatbreads in Iran. I was nervous about trying new foods when we first came to Brisbane. The food was unlike anything I had eaten back home. Now, I love it! Hamburgers, vegemite on toast, and grilled kangaroo are my favorites.

I like to share pictures of Australian festivals and events on my Instagram. I took this photo of the poppies on Anzac Day. It is a local holiday. I did not know about it until I got to Brisbane. Anzac Day takes place on April 25 each year. It is held in honor of all the Australians who have died in war and military duty.

A New School

Education is a big part of life in Iran. All children in Iran go to school for at least nine years. Parents want the best future for their children, and they often pay for their children to take extra classes after school.

Detention centers in the South Pacific, however, do not have good schools. There are few supplies and few qualified teachers. Some centers do not have schools at all. In these places, children go to local schools instead. Refugee children often do not feel safe in these schools. They are bullied by locals. Some schools even hurt children for poor behavior. For Iranian refugees, it is difficult to adjust to this after receiving a good education in their homeland.

Education is important in Iran and in Australia. In both countries, students begin school at age six. They attend until they are 18 in Iran, or at least 16 in Australia.

UN Rights of the Child

You have the right to a good quality education. You should be encouraged to go to school to the highest level you can.

Many schools have special programs to help refugee children. They have tutors, translation services, after-school programs, classes to help students learn English, and more.

Like Iran, Australia has a good education system. In fact, the country has some of the best schools in the world. Students there get a lot of support from their teachers. There are programs for children who need more help, and for those who do very well in their studies and are able to learn extra ideas. Children go to school for 13 years. They can also take part in extracurricular activities such as sports, arts, and technology programs.

Refugee children often face many challenges when they first arrive at their new school in Australia. Some did not go to school while they were living in centers, and are behind in their studies. They may not speak English. This makes it difficult for them to study and to make friends. Newcomers may feel as though they do not fit in at school because they have a different culture, eat different foods, and dress differently.

Zahra's Story: A New Way of Learning

It was so difficult to fit in at school in Brisbane. It was hard to make friends because I did not know how to speak English. I also had trouble keeping up with the teacher and the other kids. My parents were disappointed with my grades. I had done so well in Iran. They wanted the same for me in Brisbane. But English is so different from **Arabic**. My father put me in an after-school program so I could learn English quickly. It helped a lot.

I practiced during evenings and on weekends because I did not want to let my family down. They believed so strongly in giving me a good education. They hoped I could go to university one day, and I am finally there. I am in my first year in the international studies program at the University of Queensland!

In Iran, boys and girls go to separate schools. There are even different textbooks for boys and girls.

Story in Numbers

In Iran, about

58 percent

of the people enroll in university. About

37 percent

of Australians go to university.

20

Dear Yasmin,
I had the best grades in my class when I graduated. I earned a full **scholarship** to university. I could not have afforded to go otherwise. I am so thankful that I can choose to study any subject I want. I know you wanted to be an engineer or an accountant. I am sorry that universities in Iran are now banning women from studying engineering or accounting. I know you worked very hard in school and hoped things would change when the president was elected. I hope they still do one day.
Zahra

In Iran, I did not have the same opportunities as my brother. The government does not want to educate girls. They think women should focus on their families, not work. I am lucky that in Australia, boys and girls are treated as equals.

My mother believes all children should have the best chance at success in their lives. She knows how hard it was for me and my sister when we first arrived here. We would not have made it through our first year at our new school without the help of others. Now, my mother wants to give back. She has started tutoring refugee students on weekends. I help her when I have time away from my studies, too.

Isfahan University in Iran and many other Iranian universities view subjects, such as computer science and engineering, as being better suited to men than women. Traditionally, men work in these fields and many companies do not want to hire women.

21

Everything Changes

There is little support for refugees in detention centers in the South Pacific. The conditions in these centers are harsh. There is not enough food, and health care is poor. There are not enough **counselors** to help refugees overcome the terrible experiences they had in their homeland and at the center. The conditions in these centers are getting worse. The **United Nations High Commissioner for Refugees (UNHCR)** processes refugee applications. It often makes trips to detention centers and has said they should be shut down due to the poor conditions. It has asked the Australian government to take refugees out of the centers. The Australian government has not made any plans to do so.

Refugees who are resettled in Australia have a very different experience. They receive a lot of support. Before arriving in Australia, they take a five-day course. This teaches them about life in their host country.

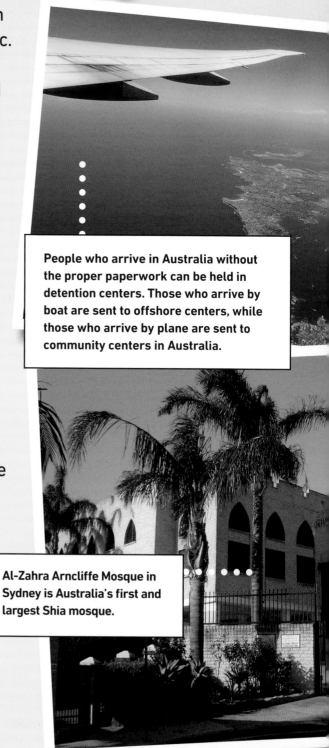

People who arrive in Australia without the proper paperwork can be held in detention centers. Those who arrive by boat are sent to offshore centers, while those who arrive by plane are sent to community centers in Australia.

Al-Zahra Arncliffe Mosque in Sydney is Australia's first and largest Shia mosque.

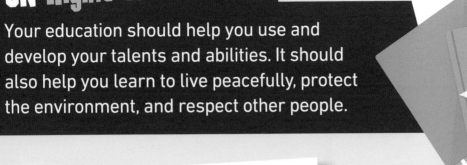

UN Rights of the Child

Your education should help you use and develop your talents and abilities. It should also help you learn to live peacefully, protect the environment, and respect other people.

Public health care is provided for free or at a low cost to all Australians.

Refugees can get help setting up a bank account, finding a doctor, and using public transportation. Families with children are helped with childcare while they are at work. Refugees can apply for counseling. Translators help refugees fill out forms.

In Australia, there are many Muslim communities. Refugee families from Iran can meet and make friends in mosques. But even simple tasks can be difficult in a new country. For example, a refugee may not know the city transportation routes well enough to find their way around. They may not be able to ask for help if they do not know the local language.

Zahra's Story: My New Way of Life

When we arrived in Brisbane, we lived in an apartment owned by the government. We were allowed to live there while my parents found jobs. After about a year, we looked for our own home. We rented an apartment in a mostly Muslim neighborhood for a few years. There was a mosque and some **Halal** restaurants nearby. Finally, we saved enough money to buy our own home. We stayed in the same neighborhood because we had made so many friends there.

Christmas events take place at South Bank in Brisbane. They include fireworks, carolers, lights, and more.

Story in Numbers

In 2011, there were

34,453

people who were born in Iran living in Australia.

The streets are so peaceful in Brisbane. Many others in my community share my beliefs. Christmas and Easter are very important holidays in Australia. They are not celebrated in Iran. I have learned about them from my friends. I enjoy the spirit of the season and the joy people spread to others.

1

Dear Yasmin,
I have seen on the news that things are getting worse in the centers in the South Pacific. I wish there was something I could do. I am scared to hold a rally or write a blog after what happened to my brother. But all my friends here say we are free to speak our minds in Australia. They have said they will help me protest. It is great to know they care. Zahra

Brisbane's Queensland Art Gallery | Gallery of Modern Art (QAGOMA) is home to more than 17,000 works of art.

I also enjoy visiting local museums and art galleries. When I first came to Brisbane, it was a good way to learn about my new country. I love sharing my culture with my friends, too. On special holidays, I cook meals for them. Some have even come to my mosque. They let me show them how to put on a hijab.

My friend, Amira, has been my biggest supporter. Her family came to Brisbane as refugees from Iraq. She helped me meet new people and appreciate life in Brisbane. We go to the same university. She wants to be a human rights lawyer.

Zahra's Story: Looking to the Future

Settling in Brisbane was a big adjustment. My parents used a government program to find work. It helps people prepare for interviews, write a resume, and look for work. At first, my parents took whatever jobs they could get. But they took classes to learn English and also enrolled in programs that help them have their skills recognized in Australia. Now, my mother works as a teacher. My father is a supervisor at a meat-processing plant.

Shortly after we arrived, my brother got into the University of Queensland to finish his degree. Now, he has a job as an engineer.

Australia is home to about 25 million people who have come from all over the world.

UN Rights of the Child

You have the right to find out things and share what you think with others, by talking, drawing, writing, or in any other way, unless it harms or offends other people.

Gold Coast University Hospital in Southport is one of the largest teaching and research centers in Queensland. Griffith University has a campus near the hospital.

I want to work in the government so I can help change immigration policies. My favorite class is women's studies. Women are often not treated as equals in Iran. I want to find ways to help, especially since most of my family still lives in my homeland.

Anahita is about to start medical school at Griffith University in Brisbane. We are all so proud of her.

I have now lived in Brisbane for longer than I lived in Iran. But Australia's laws are changing. Boat people are not resettled at all now. Australia says it does not have the means to help everyone that arrives. Some people are afraid of Muslim cultures. In New Zealand, a man shot and killed 51 people at two mosques. I know things like that are rare, though. Most people are very kind and accepting of our culture. So many people have helped us build a new life here. For that, I am forever grateful.

Dear Yasmin,
I wish you could come to Australia. I worry that changes to Australia's immigration policies may make it impossible. Australia is not as open to newcomers as it once was. I am glad we arrived so long ago. I worry, too, about the people stuck in detention centers and those who have become stranded. I wish I could help. Zahra

Do Not Forget Our Stories!

Life in Iran is becoming harder. There are not enough jobs, food, or water for everyone. The government takes away people's rights and freedoms. It wants to force people to live only a traditional Islamic culture. Learning English has been banned from public schools. People who protest are punished. Many Iranians hope to flee to Australia.

Not everyone welcomes newcomers to their country. Iranians are sometimes treated poorly. **Islamophobia** is a growing problem. Some people wrongly believe that refugees with different cultures and beliefs threaten their own ways of life. Others believe refugees take jobs from locals, or live only on money from the government.

Refugees enrich their host countries by bringing their cultures from their homelands. They share them with their new communities.

UN Rights of the Child

You have the right to help if you have been hurt, neglected, or badly treated.

Many Australians take part in anti-racism events to show their support for newcomers to the country.

In truth, refugees contribute a lot to society. They bring much needed skills into the country and take jobs that may not otherwise be filled. They pay **taxes** and purchase goods. Iranians and other refugees build strong communities in their host countries. They hope to build a positive future for themselves and their families. People in host countries can look for ways to support newcomers so they feel safe, respected, and welcome.

Discussion Prompts

1. Why does Australia place refugees in detention centers on nearby islands? Why do some people protest this?
2. How are people's rights and freedoms limited in Iran?
3. What support is available for refugees in Australia?

Glossary

Arabic Relating to the language and culture of Arabs

blog A website or page that is regularly updated

caseworkers People employed to provide help in a community

counselors People who help others with personal problems

crisis payment A sum of money given in times of great need

culture The shared beliefs, values, customs, traditions, arts, and ways of life of a particular group of people

detention center Place where people who have illegally entered a country are kept

ethnic groups Groups of people who have the same culture or religious origin

Halal Meat that Muslims can eat

hijab Head covering scarf worn by Muslim women in public

homeland The country where someone was born or grew up

host country A country that offers to give refugees a home

immigration policies Rules set by a government about who can and cannot move to a country

Islamophobia A fear or dislike of Muslims

LGBTQ Stands for lesbian, gay, bisexual, transgender, and queer

refugee A person who flees from his or her own country to another due to unsafe conditions

refugee status To be legally labeled as a refugee

resettled Settled in a new place

rights Privileges and freedoms protected by law

scholarship A payment made to support education

smuggler A person who moves people or things illegally

taxes Money paid to a government for services such as road maintenance

terrorism Use of violence to force people to accept a point of view

trade Purchase and sale of goods

United Nations High Commissioner for Refugees (UNHCR) A program that protects and supports refugees everywhere

Learning More

Books

Hudak, Heather C. *Immigration and Refugees.* Crabtree Publishing Company, 2019.

Leatherdale, Mary Beth. *Stormy Seas: Stories of Young Boat Refugees.* Annick Press, 2017.

Wallace, Sandra Neil, and Rich Wallace. *First Generation: 36 Trailblazing Immigrants and Refugees Who Make America Great.* Little, Brown Books for Young Readers, 2018.

Websites

https://www.cia.gov/library/publications/the-world-factbook/geos/ir.html
Learn all about Iran and its history, people, economy, and culture.

https://kids.nationalgeographic.com/explore/countries/iran/#iran-market.jpg
Find out more about the history, government, and people of Iran.

www.refugeecouncil.org.au/statistics
Get the facts and figures about refugees coming to Australia.

www.unicef.org/rightsite/files/uncrcchilldfriendlylanguage.pdf
Learn more about the UN Convention on the Rights of the Child.

Index

About the Author

Heather C. Hudak has written hundreds of books for children and edited thousands more. She loves learning about new topics, traveling the world, and spending time with her husband and many pets.